GA

CENGAGE Learning

Novels for Students, Volume 28

Project Editor: Ira Mark Milne Rights Acquisition and Management: Jermaine Bobbitt, Vernon English, Leitha Etheridge-Sims, Sara Teller Composition: Evi Abou-El-Seoud Manufacturing: Drew Kalasky

Imaging: Lezlie Light

Product Design: Pamela A. E. Galbreath, Jennifer Wahi Content Conversion: Civie Green, Katrina Coach Product Manager: Meggin Condino © 2009 Gale, Cengage Learning

For product information and technology assistance, contact us at **Gale Customer Support, 1-800-877-4253.**

For permission to use material from this text or product, submit all requests online at **www.cengage.com/permissions**.

Further permissions questions can be emailed to **permissionrequest@cengage.com** While every effort has been made to ensure the reliability of the information presented in this publication, Gale, a part of Cengage Learning, does not guarantee the accuracy of the data contained herein. Gale accepts no payment for listing; and inclusion in the publication of any organization, agency, institution, publication, service, or individual does not imply endorsement of the editors or publisher. Errors brought to the attention of the publisher and verified to the satisfaction of the publisher will be corrected in future editions.

Gale
27500 Drake Rd.
Farmington Hills, MI, 48331-3535

ISBN-13: 978-0-7876-8685-7
ISBN-10: 0-7876-8685-9
ISSN 1094-3552

This title is also available as an e-book.

ISBN-13: 978-1-4144-3832-0
ISBN-10: 1-4144-3832-X
Contact your Gale, a part of Cengage Learning sales
representative for ordering information.

Printed in the United States of America
1 2 3 4 5 6 7 13 12 11 10 09

Cannery Row

John Steinbeck

1945

Introduction

Cannery Row, which was published in 1945, is composed of portraits of the title location's inhabitants. It evokes the fish canning district in Monterey, California, in the early 1940s. Although the novel takes place during World War II, the only hint of war is the brief mention of soldiers stationed nearby and a snapshot of two soldiers and their dates. This omission is perhaps explained by the fact that Steinbeck wrote *Cannery Row* in response to his dissatisfaction upon his return from the battlefields as a newspaper reporter.

The characters in *Cannery Row* are often troubled, and they experience a great deal of conflict, misery, violence, pain, and grief. Nevertheless, they experience a social harmony in the vicissitudes and torments of life at peace amid the horrors of a distant war. This gave the novel vitality when it appeared. Steinbeck did not write another protest novel like *The Grapes of Wrath.* Instead, he wrote a book that portrayed a spirit of peace and community. That spirit still can be felt in the book and is enhanced by the fact that the novel is now a period piece that nevertheless remains true to characteristics that are essentially and timelessly human.

Cannery Row is a series of thirty-two free-standing chapters (vignettes) that are connected yet independent, which is a point that Steinbeck also makes about nature in the novel. In the prologue, Steinbeck asks how he can convey what Cannery Row is like. He answers using an analogy drawn from the way marine animals are collected, a fitting one since Doc makes his living gathering marine creatures. "When you collect marine animals, there are certain flat worms so delicate," Steinbeck explains "that they are almost impossible to capture whole, for they break and tatter under the touch. You must let them ooze and crawl of their will onto a knife blade and then lift them gently into your bottle of sea water. And perhaps that might be," Steinbeck suggests, "the way to write this book—to open the page and let the stories crawl in by themselves."

A recent edition of *Cannery Row* appears in *Steinbeck: Novels 1942-1952*, which was published in 2001.

Author Biography

John Steinbeck was born February 27, 1902, in Salinas, California, the third of four children, and the only boy. His father, John Steinbeck, Sr., managed a flour mill and was Monterey County Treasurer. His mother, Olive Hamilton Steinbeck, had been a schoolteacher before she married. The family lived a cultured, comfortable life in a large Victorian house and passed summers in their Pacific Grove cottage or at Steinbeck's uncle's ranch.

While in high school, Steinbeck almost died of pleural pneumonia. While convalescing, he began writing stories. After graduation, Steinbeck enrolled at Stanford University as an English major but left without a degree in 1925, having taken several leaves in order to work as a mountain surveyor in Big Sur, California, and as a carpenter's apprentice in a sugar mill, where he also supervised day laborers and performed chemical tests on sugar beets.

In 1926, while in New York City, Steinbeck worked on the construction crew building Madison Square Garden and was a reporter for the *New York American*. Failing to sell his fiction, Steinbeck returned to California. In 1929, his novel *Cup of Gold* was published. In 1930, Steinbeck married Carol Henning, the first of his three wives. Also that year, he met Edward F. Ricketts, the marine biologist and the owner of the Pacific Biological

Laboratory who became the model for Doc (the protagonist of 1945's *Cannery Row*). *Tortilla Flat*, published in 1935, brought Steinbeck fame. He published *Of Mice and Men* in 1937 and *The Grapes of Wrath* in 1939. Bestsellers, both became highly successful movies. *The Grapes of Wrath* won the Pulitzer Prize in 1940 and was also banned by many libraries and condemned in the U.S. Congress by Oklahoma representative Lyle Borden for its denunciation of the inequities of capitalism.

In 1940, Steinbeck went on a marine collecting expedition with Ricketts in the Gulf of California. Later that year, he went to Mexico with his first wife to work on the screenplay for *The Forgotten Village*. Steinbeck also met President Franklin D. Roosevelt and discussed propaganda initiatives against Nazi Germany. In 1941, Steinbeck separated from his first wife and began living with Gwyn Conger, a singer with whom he had begun an affair in 1939 and whom he then married in 1943. In 1942, on assignment for the Army Air Forces to write a book about training bomber crews, Steinbeck visited air bases throughout the United States. In 1943, Steinbeck became a war correspondent for the *New York Tribune*. He returned to New York with battle fatigue and a burst ear drum. Also in 1943, Steinbeck wrote the story that served as the basis for the screenplay for Alfred Hitchcock's film *Lifeboat*. Although he did not win, Steinbeck was nominated for an Academy Award for best screenplay in 1944, the year he wrote *Cannery Row*.

In August of 1944, Steinbeck and Conger had a son, Thomas; two years later, in June 1946, they had another son whom they named John. In October, Steinbeck and Conger visited Sweden, Denmark, France, and Norway. In Norway, Steinbeck was awarded the King Haakon Liberty Cross. In 1947, Steinbeck wrote *The Pearl*, a tragic morality tale set in Bolivia about longing and greed. That year, he also traveled to the Soviet Union with the photographer Robert Capa. Their collaboration, *The Russian Journal*, was published in 1948. That same year, Conger filed for a divorce, and Ed Ricketts died. Distraught, Steinbeck nevertheless began work on two projects, the screenplay for the Elia Kazan/Marlon Brando film, *Viva Zapata!*, and the novel *East of Eden*. In 1950, Steinbeck married Elaine Scott. In 1954, he published *Sweet Thursday*, the sequel to *Cannery Row*.

While Steinbeck continued to write novels, a travel book, and newspaper columns, he also undertook a number of "good-will" missions for the U.S. government throughout Western Europe and within the Soviet bloc. He wrote speeches for democratic presidential candidate Adlai Stevenson in 1960, traveled to Europe on behalf of President John F. Kennedy, and wrote parts of Lyndon Johnson's inaugural address. In 1962, he was awarded the Nobel Prize for Literature. Steinbeck, unlike many American writers, supported the Vietnam War. He traveled extensively in Vietnam, even going into battle alongside American forces, and reported back to President Johnson. On December 20, 1968, after a series of strokes and heart attacks, Steinbeck died at home in New York City. Six days later, his ashes were buried in a plot in the Garden of Memories Cemetery in Salinas, California.

Prologue

Fishing boats return to Cannery Row at dawn. People arrive for work at the canneries. The narrator wonders how to present his story.

Chapter 1

Lee Chong rents a large storage shed to Mack and his friends to live in for five dollars a week. From their doorway, Mack and the boys can see across the way into Doc's windows. They want to do something nice for Doc.

Chapter 2

Steinbeck meditates on the value and the costs of worldly success.

Chapter 3

William, a former bouncer at Dora Flood's brothel, is unable to make friends with Mack and the boys. He stabs himself to death with an ice-pick, on a dare, after his confession that he felt like killing himself was ignored or mocked by Dora, by one of the prostitutes, and by the cook at the brothel.

Chapter 4

A mysterious Chinese man "disappeared among the piles and steel posts which support the piers" every evening and reappeared each dawn carrying a "wicker basket." The children, who usually taunt odd characters, are afraid of him. But one child, Andy, taunts him with a racial rhyme. As he does, he is gripped with a sense of lonely fear that causes him to see a vast, hallucinatory, and weird landscape.

Media Adaptations

- In 1982, David S. Ward directed a film version of *Cannery Row* that combines *Cannery Row* and its sequel, *Sweet Thursday*. The film stars Nick Nolte as Doc and Debra Winger as Suzy. It was produced by Chai Productions and distributed by

Chapter 5

Doc's laboratory and living quarters are filled with preserved marine and animal specimens. There are prints on the wall and shelves of books. Doc knows the complexities of nature and the spiritual and intellectual delights of art, culture, and scholarship. He is a teacher for the odd souls populating Cannery Row.

Chapter 6

Doc collects marine animals. Hazel, one of the men living at the Palace Flophouse, assists him. They gossip about Gay, who has moved into the Flophouse to get away from his wife, and about Henri, a painter who is building a boat that he lives in but never finishes. Doc explains that Henri likes boats but does not like sailing.

Chapter 7

Mack and the boys turn the Flophouse into a home, crowding it with discarded furniture and a great chrome-decorated cookstove. Eddie, who sometimes works as a bartender, brings leftover liquor back to the Flophouse. Mack and the boys decide to throw a party for Doc and to collect hundreds of frogs for him.

Chapter 8

Mr. and Mrs. Sam Malloy live in the vacant lot between Lee Chong's store and the Flophouse, in a discarded boiler from a local cannery factory. They quarrel when she wants to hang curtains and he cannot understand why since "we got no windows." She complains men do not understand women; he rubs her back until she falls asleep.

Chapter 9

Mack offers to gather frogs for Doc at a nickel a frog. Doc agrees, but will not lend Mack his car. Doc must drive to La Jolla to collect octopi. Mack thinks Lee Chong will let them use his truck. Doc gives Mack a note for Red Williams at the gas station authorizing Red to fill their tank with ten gallons. Lee Chong's truck is broken but Gay fixes it.

Chapter 10

The boy, Frankie, has been expelled from school. He hangs around the edges of Doc's laboratory. After three weeks, he approaches Doc's worktable. He tells Doc he is beaten at home by the men who come to see his mother, or they give him a nickel and send him away. Doc has him wash his filthy hands, clips and cleans his lice-infested hair, and shows Frankie how to sort fish specimens by size, although the task is daunting for him. When Doc has guests, Frankie accidentally spills a tray full of beer on one. He retreats to the cellar, curls up in a box of excelsior, and whimpers. Doc follows him, hears his whimpers, and goes back upstairs because "there wasn't a thing in the world he could do."

Chapter 11

Gay fixes Lee Chong's Model T, and the men set out to catch frogs. Mack tries to get Red Williams to put five instead of ten gallons in the tank and give him change in cash. Red, warned of Mack's tricks by Doc, refuses.

The Model T will not take hills in first gear. But it can, turned backwards, in reverse. The needle valve of the carburetor breaks; Gay takes it to get it fixed. The car he hitches in breaks down. Gay fixes it. The grateful owner takes him to a bar. After a drunken brawl, Gay is arrested and put in the county jail, a comfortable place, where he stays for six months. When Gay does not return, Eddie hikes over to a construction site to see if he can find a Model T to steal a carburetor needle from.

Chapter 12

Monterey can boast about its concern for the honor of its writers. After embalming the body of the American humorist Josh Billings, the embalmer tossed the organs into the bay. A boy and his dog found the liver and intestines and would have used them for fishing bait had not an alert man passing noticed they were dragging what looked like a man's liver. The embalmer was made to collect and clean the parts, put them in a leaden box, and bury them inside the coffin with the body.

Chapter 13

Eddie returns before dawn with a carburetor. In the morning, the boys set out and reach a sandy edge of the Carmel River. They decide to wait till nightfall to catch frogs. They nap. Hazel cooks a rooster they have run over. The owner of the land approaches with his gun and dog. He orders them off his property. Mack ingratiates himself, addressing the man as Captain, by praising his pointer. The man agrees it is a fine dog but notes that Nola (the dog) is ill from an infected wound. Mack asks to look at Nola's wound, immediately makes friends with her, and when Mack suggests an Epsom salts compress, the Captain asks him to go home with him to tend to the dog. Mack tells the others to clean up the campsite.

Chapter 14

Early morning, Cannery Row hardly stirring, two soldiers and their girls walk tired and happy through the streets. The girls are wearing the boys' hats; the boys have their dates' hats on. They stop on the beach, drink some beer and the soldiers lay their heads in their girls' laps. A watchman comes to shoo them away, but one of the soldiers smiles at the watchman and tells him, colorfully, to get lost, and the watchman does.

Chapter 15

Mack treats the dog. The Captain offers him one of her litter and goes frog-catching with the boys in his own pond. They catch hundreds of frogs. Since the Captain's wife is away, they get drunk together, and the boys leave for home glad they are doing something nice for Doc.

Chapter 16

Dora and the prostitutes take care of the sick during an outbreak of influenza and at a time when the brothel is exceptionally busy because a new regiment of soldiers has arrived at the nearby army base. The canneries are employing as many workers as possible because of a bountiful sardine catch, which also helps to keep the brothel busy.

Chapter 17

Even when he sees the curtains drawn and hears Gregorian chant being played on the phonograph, and knows Doc has a woman with him, Mack is sensitive to Doc's loneliness. Doc drives to La Jolla for octopi. Mack and the boys are collecting frogs. Henri, from Red Williams's gas station, watches a flagpole skater who has installed himself atop the flagpole at Hollman's Department Store. Doc stops for food and picks up a hitchhiker. He stops for a beer and asks the hitchhiker if he wants one. When the hitchhiker lectures Doc about drinking and driving, Doc orders him out of the car. Curious to see what it tastes like, Doc orders a beer milk shake, telling the waitress he is sick and drinks it on his doctor's orders, having discovered that people prefer lies to the truth.

Chapter 18

Collecting octopi, Doc discovers a drowned girl underwater. Shaken by the sight, he tells a passing stranger. The stranger says he will get a bounty when he reports it. Doc leaves in disgust, telling the stranger to make the police report and take the bounty himself.

Chapter 19

Dr. Merrivale shoots an air gun at the flagpole skater. Richard Frost cannot figure out how the flagpole skater goes to the toilet. Driven from his bed by curiosity one night, he calls out the question to the skater on his perch and learns, as he tells his wife when he gets home and slips back into bed, that "he's got a can up there."

Chapter 20

Mack and the boys return the truck to Lee Chong and make a deal to trade frogs for groceries. The Flophouse gang decide to have the party for Doc at Doc's lab because Doc has a record player and because they can surprise him when he returns.

They decorate Doc's place and bring over the crate of frogs. They begin the party without Doc, and it ends after one in the morning, but before Doc's return. The party turns into a melee. The case of frogs is broken open and all the frogs escape. The place is a mess and the damage is considerable.

Chapter 21

In the morning Doc returns, exhausted. The lab is a shambles; animals are in panic; records, phonograph, glass cases, and instruments are broken. Mack, waiting for Doc, admits the mess is his making. Doc punches him in the jaw twice and calls on him to fight; Mack says he had "it coming." Once his anger is spent, Doc calmly asks Mack to tell him what happened. Mack explains that they planned a surprise party for him, thinking he would be back in time for it, but that it "got out of hand." Mack tells Doc he is sorry and adds that saying that "don't do no good," and that he has been "sorry all my life," and that whenever he tries to do something good it turns out badly. He promises Doc that he and the boys will pay for the damage and clean up the place. Doc tells him that even though he means to pay, he never will and that he [Doc] needs to clean up by himself. Mack leaves. Doc has forgiven him.

Chapter 22

Henri lives in his boat, often with a female companion. His girlfriends keep moving out because the cabin is too small. One night, alone, feeling sorry for himself, Henri sees a handsome young man and a beautiful boy sitting across from him. The man cuts the baby's throat with a straight razor. Henri goes over to Doc's place in fright, hoping Doc will go back to the boat with him to see if he sees what Henri saw. Doc declines, explaining it will not help Henri whether Doc sees the apparition or not. As they talk, a woman visitor appears. She has a date with Doc. Doc tells Henri to tell her his story. She goes home with Henri and stays for five months until she moves out, like the others, because of the cramped quarters.

Chapter 23

After the party at the lab, "gloom settled over the Palace Flophouse." Mack takes to his bed. The boys are ostracized by everyone in Cannery Row. Only the dog, Darling, seems to keep her cheer. The rest of the town also suffers. The Malloys fight. A group of women effect the temporary closing of Dora's brothel. Doc has to borrow money to pay for the damages to the lab. One of the townsmen loses his legs when he falls asleep on the railroad tracks and a train runs over him. The town loses convention business because the brothel is closed. Some boats get free of their moorings and are tossed, broken, onto the beach.

The gloom begins to lift when Darling gets sick. Hazel and Jones go to see if Doc can help. He protests he is not a veterinarian, but he looks at

Darling and prescribes a course of treatment. Following his instructions, the boys take the dog through her illness and restore her to health. With her return to health, everything in Cannery Row begins to get better. The brothel is allowed to reopen. Lee Chong resumes friendly relations with the boys.

Mack visits Dora and tells her how the party was actually a result of good intentions, no matter how badly it turned out, and asks her what he can do for Doc. Her answer—"You gave him a party he didn't get to. Why don't you give him a party he does get to"—greatly impresses Mack and sets the direction for the final section of the book.

Doc and Richard Frost drink beer on the Fourth of July, waiting for the parade to come by. Across the way, they see the Flophouse guys sitting outside their door. Doc compares them to people driven by ambition, and considers the boys to be truly the wise men of the age in their detachment.

Chapter 24

Mary Talbot is rumored to be descended from witches. Sometimes she has alley cats to tea. She loves to give parties. Her husband, Tom, is a writer who lives on hope even as his stories are rejected by major magazines. Finally, he is overcome by despair at his failure. When Mary sees one of the cats in the yard tormenting a mouse, and screams, Tom kills the mouse and shoos the cat away. Through this divertissement he escapes his gloom.

Mary says she understands how cats are, but she will have difficulty liking the predatory cat. The chapter ends with the suggestion that she is pregnant.

Chapter 25

Good cheer spreads throughout Cannery Row. The boys decide to give Doc another surprise party, but not to force it to happen. They decide, too, that they need an occasion for the party. Mack goes over to Doc's to find out when his birthday is. Not wanting to make him suspicious, he leads up to his question with talk about astrology and horoscopes. But Doc recognizes a ploy and suspects a hidden motive and says October 27 is his birthday when, in fact, it is December 18.

Chapter 26

Joey's father killed himself with rat poison after a year of unemployment. Willard taunts and teases him and challenges him to fight without being able to get a rise out of him or compromising Joey's dignity.

Chapter 27

Mack and the boys make preparations for the party. No one is formally invited; the news of the party just spreads through Cannery Row. Everybody prepares for it. The women at Dora's make Doc a silk patchwork quilt out of old lingerie.

Mack and the boys decide to have the party at Doc's, but not if he does not show up. Doc overhears a drunk in a bar mention it. Realizing that everyone will bring liquor but no one will think of food, he buys food as well as wine and whiskey. As a gift, Mack and the boys trap tomcats for Doc, and keep them at the Flophouse. Although the cats are caged, they make Darling skittery.

Chapter 28

Frankie sees a clock in a jewelry store window and longs to give to Doc. He breaks the window at night and flees with the clock and is apprehended. Despite Doc's request that Frankie be paroled in his custody, Frankie is confined to a mental hospital.

Chapter 29

The afternoon of the party, Doc finishes his work, locks away valuable, breakable, or dangerous objects and animals, and takes a shower. Mack and the boys bathe and decide not to bring the cats over to the lab. The prostitutes dress in street frocks rather than in the elaborate gowns of their trade. Everyone waits for the time of the party to begin.

Chapter 30

The party is a ritual release of repressed energy in celebration of life's messiness; it is a great success, with eating, drinking, dancing, noise, and festive brawling. Even the police, called by a woman five blocks away because of the noise, stay to take part. The squad car is commandeered for a liquor run. At the center of the chapter, Doc reads a Sanskrit poem in translation about lost love.

Chapter 31

A gopher finds a perfect spot to make his home, far from gardens, so that there is no fear of traps. After burrowing a fine domicile beneath the earth, the gopher waits for a female companion. When none arrives and the gopher grows lonely, he seeks a mate at another gopher hole only to be attacked by the male gopher who lives in it. The injured gopher returns to his home, but when no female companion appears, he moves "to a dahlia garden where they put out traps every night."

Chapter 32

Doc is in a melancholy mood. Amid his caged specimens of rats and rattlesnakes, he eats, listens to Gregorian chant, and looks at the poem he read at the party, reciting lines that celebrate the illumination brought to the poet by his past, now lost, experiences.

Horace Abbeville

Horace Abbeville is a minor character who deeds over a building to Lee Chong in order to pay off a cash debt. Lee Chong allows Mack and the boys to live in it. They call it the Palace Flophouse and Grill.

Alfred

Alfred is the watchman and bouncer at Dora Flood's brothel, the Bear Flag Restaurant.

Andy

Andy is a boy who teases the mysterious Old Chinaman, and as he chants his racially disparaging rhyme, he experiences a frightening hallucination.

Captain

This is what Mack calls the man who comes to shoo Mack and his friends off his land when they are camping out waiting to catch frogs. The man is won over when Mack takes care of his ailing dog. He lets them catch frogs in his pond, and, since his wife is away, the house is a mess and he and the boys get drunk.

Mr. Carriaga

Carriaga appears in an anecdote about an actual writer, the American humorist Josh Billings. He discovers that, after Billings's body was embalmed, the embalmer threw Billings's organs into the bay.

Kitty Casini

Kitty Casini is a cat that Mary Talbot has befriended. Mary is disturbed when she sees the cat tormenting a mouse.

Lee Chong

Lee Chong is a Chinese grocer who owns the general store. He is a shrewd but honorable businessman, hard-nosed on the one hand, yet good-hearted and even generous on the other.

Darling

Darling is a dog that Mack and the boys adopt as a puppy and care for. She is loved by all of them. Darling serves, in the plot, to bring Mack and the boys back into the community of Cannery Row after the disastrous party they throw at Doc's.

Doc

Doc is the hero and central figure of *Cannery Row*. There is an air of integrity, melancholy wisdom, and stoicism about him. He runs a biological laboratory and collects marine specimens that he sells to experimental laboratories. He is a popular and loved figure, yet he is still lonely. He respects the boundaries between individuals but also is attentive to all human need. Despite his title of "Doc," he is not a physician. Nevertheless, when necessary, he attends to human patients and to sick animals.

Eddie

Eddie sometimes lives at the Flophouse. He works as a replacement bartender and keeps jugs behind the bar and fills them with a mix of leftover drinks to bring back to the Flophouse.

Eric

Eric is a barber, a friend of Henri the painter. He gives Doc a rowing machine as a birthday present.

Flagpole Skater

As an advertising ploy, this man skates on a platform built atop a flagpole outside Hollman's Department Store.

Eva Flanegan

Eva Flanegan is one of the prostitutes at Dora Flood's. She attends church and tends to drink.

When William, Dora's bouncer, tells her he feels like killing himself, her response is to yell at him and berate him.

Dora Flood

Dora Flood runs the brothel on Cannery Row. She is a tough and shrewd businesswoman but also a good boss and an active and willing participant in the community. This is illustrated best by Dora having the women who work for her sit by the bedsides of the sick during an influenza epidemic, but it is also illustrated by the amount of her charitable contributions—necessarily large payoffs because her business is illegal.

Frankie

Frankie is a troubled boy who does not attend school. His mother is sexually promiscuous, perhaps even an independent prostitute. The men who visit her either hit the boy or give him a nickel to leave. Frankie is drawn to Doc and hangs around his lab trying to be helpful. He steals a clock to give to Doc but is caught and sent to an asylum.

Richard Frost

Richard Frost appears briefly as a drinking companion with whom Doc bets that Mack and the boys will not even glance at the Fourth of July parade as it passes.

Gay

Gay moves into the Flophouse because of difficulties with his wife. He beats her and she hits him while he is asleep. He is an excellent mechanic. He spends most of the time in the county jail for having committed drunken mischief.

The Greek

He is the cook at the brothel. When William tells him he feels like killing himself, the Greek does not think he really means it and hands him the ice pick with which, to the Greek's troubled astonishment, William stabs himself.

Hazel

Hazel is a man. He was the last of seven children and his overburdened mother did not discover his gender until after she had named him. He lives at the Palace Flophouse. He is a simple man who asks Doc questions because he likes being spoken to.

Henri

Henri is a painter, but he does not paint. He makes art out of chicken feathers or broken nutshells or pins and pincushions. A Francophile, he is not French and his name is not really Henri. He lives in a boat he is always building and never completes. In a disturbed moment, he hallucinates a man slitting a child's throat. He is fascinated by the flagpole skater.

The Hitchhiker

When Doc stops for a beer, the hitchhiker to whom he is giving a lift lectures him about the dangers of drinking and driving. Doc orders him out of the car.

Hughie

He lives at the Palace Flophouse.

Mr. Jacobs

He owns the jewelry store from which Frankie steals the clock to give to Doc.

Joey

Joey is a gentle boy. His father committed suicide and Willard teases him about it.

Jones

He lives at the Palace Flophouse.

Mack

Mack is one of the principle characters of the novel. He is a loser in terms of social success and his projects often go terribly wrong. Still, he is a good-hearted, generous man, rough but tender. He lives in the Flophouse and is paterfamilias to the other men living there.

Phylis Mae

She is one of the prostitutes at Dora's brothel.

Sam Malloy

Malloy lives in an old, discarded boiler on a vacant lot across from the Flophouse. He rents the hollow pipes in the vacant lot to hobos as places to sleep.

Mrs. Sam Malloy

Mrs. Malloy quarrels with her husband when he is insensitive to her desire to put curtains up in the windowless boiler.

McKinley Moran

Moran figures in a conversation about him between Mack and Hughie. He was a deep-sea diver, paid by the government to find buried liquor and at the same time paid by a bootlegger not to find the liquor.

Nola

Nola is the Captain's dog. Mack treats her tick wound. She is Darling's mother

An Old Chinaman

He is the mysterious figure Andy taunts. He collects things in the bay at night. One of the soles of his shoes is loose and flops as he walks.

Kitty Randolph

Kitty Randolph is a cat that Mary Talbot has befriended

Mr. Randolph

Mr. Randolph is on the board of directors of one of the canning companies. He decided to discard the old boiler in which the Malloys live.

Mr. Ryan

Ryan appears in the Josh Billings anecdote as the man Carriaga speaks to about Billings's death.

Mary Talbot

Mary is Tom's wife. She tries to keep gloom away from him, loves parties, is rumored to be the descendant of witches, and has tea parties for the neighborhood cats.

Tom Talbot

Talbot is a discouraged writer living in Cannery Row. His manuscripts come back to him with rejection notes and he is often behind in paying his bills.

Willard

Willard is a cruel boy with a streak of bully in him. He teases Joey about Joey's father, who has committed suicide.

William

William is dead at the time of the narration of *Cannery Row*. He had been the bouncer/watchman at Dora's but grew depressed because of his inability to make friends with Mack and the boys. William kills himself after complaining that he wanted to be friends and no one he told took what he said seriously.

Red Williams

Williams owns a gas station in Cannery Row.

Themes

Detachment

Although never indifferent to events or individuals, Doc has the kind of quietness about him that suggests detachment. While concerned about the welfare of others, whether the boy Frankie, the painter Henri, or the dog Darling, he also maintains a distance from others. Before treating Darling, Doc protests that he is not a vet. But once he examines the dog, he gives as good treatment as a veterinarian would. When Henri comes to him overcome by fright after his murderous hallucination, Doc keeps his distance and helps Henri by sacrificing his own pleasure for Henri's. Doc does not welcome Frankie when the boy starts to hang around his laboratory but waits until the boy has become comfortable enough to come close to him. When Frankie retreats to the cellar and remains there whimpering, Doc does not go near and comfort or support him. Rather, his attitude is reflected in the narrator's remark that "There wasn't a thing in the world he could do," reflecting the idea that fundamentally each person is alone, even when in need of another. When he cannot save Frankie from incarceration after Frankie has stolen a clock, Doc is moved, but shows it only by getting back to his work. The same idea of detachment is evident in Mack's attitude regarding the second attempt at giving Doc a party.

Overeager the first time, Mack comes to realize that he cannot force the event but must let it happen on its own. Similarly, the Flophouse boys are shown as admirable because they remain outside the excitement of the July Fourth parade. A particularly touching example of detachment is presented in the chapter concerning Joey and Willard, as Joey rebuffs Willard's bullying without responding to it. The flagpole skater represents an austere version of isolation and detachment.

Interconnectedness of All Life in Nature

Cannery Row itself, although named for the sardine canning industry located there, takes its identity not from that industry but from the particular ecology of the region, from the interconnected relationships within and between nature and culture. The natural resources of the region determine the industrial culture and that industrial culture affects the social culture. As a marine biologist, Doc depends on the natural environment as much as the canneries do. Dora and Lee Chong, too, both cater to the natural requirement for food and sexual release, respectively. In the first chapter, the narrator draws a connection between marine life and human life when he reveals his story-telling strategy. He wants his stories to "crawl" into his book "by themselves" the way "You must let" marine life "ooze and crawl … onto a knife blade and then lift them gently into your bottle of sea water." In chapter 21, Steinbeck first describes the behavior and attitudes of the animals in Doc's lab and immediately afterward describes the behavior of the people on Cannery Row. Philosophically, the narrator repeatedly draws a distinction between denatured people, people who sacrifice their natural disposition for the sake of worldly success and become ill, and people, like Mack and the boys, who remain loyal to their natures, even when the price is the lack of worldly success. Mack, for example, senses Doc's loneliness. After Mack's unsuccessful party for Doc, the whole town falls into gloom. Even Darling's health and the health of the town are linked.

Topics for Further Study

- Doc follows Frankie to the cellar in chapter 10, after the boy has accidentally spilled beer on one of the guests. Doc listens to him crying but then goes back upstairs. The narrator writes: "There wasn't a thing in the world he could do." In an essay of at least 500 words, explain why you agree or disagree with the narrator's conclusion.

- Doc makes his living by supplying animals to testing laboratories. This once-common practice has since been criticized as inhumane by many advocates of animal rights. After careful research, present a twenty-minute report to your class examining the issue of animal experimentation, its current extent, and the arguments for or against it. In cases where experimentation on animals has stopped, discuss what has replaced it and the effectiveness of the newer procedures.

- In chapter 20, the narrator reports that Lee Chong sold "felt pennants commemorating 'Fighting Bob.'" Fighting Bob refers to Robert LaFollette, Sr. (1855-1925). Using the library and the Internet for your research, prepare a fifteen-minute presentation discussing who Robert LaFollette was, what he did, and why he was important. Explain why he is mentioned in *Cannery Row*.

- Doc listens to music throughout the

novel. He is particularly fond of Gregorian chant, the music of Beethoven (he listens to the *Moonlight Sonata* and to the *Great Fugue*, commonly called by its German name, the *Grosse Fuge*), and of Maurice Ravel (he listens to the "Pavane for a Dead Princess" and to *Daphnis and Chloe*). After listening to these pieces of music yourself, prepare a lecture for your class and describe how these musical works illuminate or reflect Doc's character.

- Choose a chapter from *Cannery Row* and rewrite it so that it is narrated by Dora Flood.

Loneliness

A sense of fundamental loneliness or individual isolation runs through *Cannery Row*. Gay would rather be in jail than at home with his wife. Mrs. Malloy feels isolated in her sensibility because she is a woman. Her husband, although a good husband who comforts her, is alone in his emotional separation from her, and his goodness appears more as a result of sympathetic duty rather than real connection. The Captain wishes he were not married. Mack lives with a sense of his inability to connect with others, whether his lost wife or Doc.

The prostitutes embody loneliness and Dora has made a virtue of it in her role as a Madam. William, the brothel watchman who committed suicide, is an emblem of lonely isolation. Doc, connected as he is to nature and the life of the town, is a deeply isolated man. He lives in a flow of ever-passing experience.

Love in Varied Form

Except for Frankie's overt declaration of hopeless love for Doc, the theme of love is implicit although pervasive. There are varieties of love. With regard to the prostitutes, love appears as lust. In several situations, for Sam Malloy, for example, love appears as domestic duty. In Doc and Mack, it is shown to be a generosity of the spirit. In the Sanskrit poem Doc reads, it appears as a nebulous sense of something lost.

Respectability versus Nonconformity

Steinbeck overtly criticizes the conventions of respectability by the nature of his main characters—Doc, a loner, Mack, a loser, and Dora, a Madam. Most of the secondary characters, too—characters the reader is meant to like, whether the prostitutes, Mack's companions, Lee Chong, Henri, or the Malloys—are marginal to society and live in unconventional ways. Steinbeck also states that the qualities that are valued, like understanding, generosity, gentleness, openness, and kindness, are associated with failure. The characteristics that are associated with success are those generally held in lower esteem: "sharpness, greed, acquisitiveness, meanness, egoism, and self-interest."

Narrator as Naturalist

Not only is the force of Nature a theme of *Cannery Row*, and not only is Doc a naturalist, but the narrator of the novel is also presented as if he were a naturalist. His characters are presented as specimens that he has collected and is studying, just as Doc collects specimens and injects them with several colored fluids so that their characteristics will be highlighted and the specimens can be studied. The narrator establishes himself in the first chapter not so much as a man who makes up stories using his imagination but as a man who gathers them from the world around him.

Stereotypes

Naturalist rather than psychologist, the narrator draws characters as types rather than as individuals, and relationships as typical rather than as specific. Lee Chong is the familiar Chinese merchant, considered inscrutable and shrewd. Dora is the very portrait of a Madam with her mix of a hard exterior and a tender inside. Mr. Malloy and the Captain are stock characters, henpecked husbands. Mack is a prototypical hobo. Henri is a standard caricature of an unsuccessful artist. And Doc is an exemplary man of the first half of the twentieth century, strong, silent, self-sufficient, sensitive, in touch with nature, and yet lonely.

Vignettes

Cannery Row, a novel of approximately 130 pages, is divided into 32 chapters. Although there is a thread connecting the chapters, sometimes because of an ongoing story being told and sometimes because the events or persons described are part of the ambience of Cannery Row, each chapter is a vignette, a free-standing portrait of one or another aspect of life or nature. Even episodes in the larger story—Mack and the boys going frogging (frog hunting), or the story of Frankie—can stand alone. Chapters like those devoted to the Talbots, to the two soldiers and their girls, to the gopher, or to Josh Billings, might be removed from the book without a reader ever suspecting their absence despite the fact that their presence enriches the totality of the narrative.

Flagpole Sitting

Flagpole sitting, the practice of sitting on a small platform set upon the top of a pole for as long as possible, was a fad that reached its peak in the 1920s. Although an apparently frivolous activity, it resembles the discipline some religious hermits imposed upon themselves when they sat in isolation upon tall columns. The most famous of these is hermits St. Simeon, who sat for thirty-six years upon a column in Turkey during the first part of the fifth century C.E. Flagpole skating is a whacky variation of flagpole sitting.

The Great Depression

The exact time in which *Cannery Row* takes place is not given, but the story seems to be occurring just as the Great Depression is ending and World War II is beginning, so one can pinpoint the era as early 1940s. While the influence of the war is hardly visible in the novel, the culture of the depression is obvious. People are poor and live in makeshift dwellings. The Great Depression started at the end of 1929 when the stock market crashed. It lasted until the beginning of World War II. There was massive unemployment; people lost their homes, and itinerant poor traveled throughout the United States on railroad box-cars and lived in hobo encampments.

Taoism

Unlike the 1960s, which saw an outbreak of interest in Asian culture, Zen Buddhism, and Taoism, in 1944, when Steinbeck was writing *Cannery Row*, Taoism was quite arcane. Taoism is a Chinese philosophy of non-attachment to the things of the world. It teaches the cultivation of emptiness and the belief that any way that can be called *the* way is not the way. Its defining text is called the Tao Te Jing or the Way of Life. Its author is believed to be the Chinese sage, Lao Tse, born around 604 B.C.E.

Compare & Contrast

- **1940s:** Animals are regularly used in laboratories to develop and test medicines and cosmetics. The practice goes largely unchallenged.

  Today: The use of animals in laboratories continues, although it has become somewhat less common due to social views. Animal advocacy groups regularly protest the practice and lobby to have animal testing outlawed.

- **1940s:** Monterey is one of the major centers of fish canning.

Today: After the fishing industry collapsed in the 1950s, Monterey's Cannery Row, a street located on the waterfront, became a tourist center. It currently attracts fishermen, scuba divers, and visitors to the Monterey Bay Aquarium. Literary tourists, people drawn to Cannery Row because of Steinbeck's novel, also visit frequently.

- **1940s:** The United States recovers from the Great Depression because of the boost given to the economy (brought on by increased production in the industrial-military complex) by World War II.

  Today: The wars in Iraq and Afghanistan are draining resources from the American economy (brought on by increased military spending) and the country's infrastructure and social services suffer because of it.

World War II

Although World War II is not mentioned in *Cannery Row*, its presence haunts the book by its absence, for at the time of the novel's composition, not just the United States but the entire world was mobilized and involved in strenuous battle. The

United States, England, the Soviet Union, and their allies, fought against the Germans, the Japanese, and the Italians. *Cannery Row* presents a picture of a society that functions peacefully despite human weaknesses and conflicts. It presents a vision of the world as an organism composed by the balanced interaction of interdependent parts, a vision distinctly in contrast with the nature of war in which part is set against part as if they were not mutually dependent upon each other.

Critical Overview

Cannery Row puzzled critics when it was first published, particularly because of the circumstances of the world around it. It was written and published as World War II raged, but gave hardly a word to the war. Peter Lisca traces first responses to the novel in *The Wide World of John Steinbeck*. Lisca reports that F. O. Mathiessen, reviewing the novel in the *New York Times*, declared that "it's a puzzler why Steinbeck should have wanted to write or publish such a book at this point in his career." Lisca also states that Edmund Wilson, writing in the *New Yorker*, said that among Steinbeck's works, it was the one he "most enjoyed reading." Nevertheless, Wilson also reportedly found it "sentimental" and simple-minded in its "philosophy." Lisca further relates that the critic Orville Prescott declared that, with *Cannery Row*, Steinbeck "did not just write a trivial and seemingly meaningless and purposeless novel. He wrote with all his usual professional felicity of expression, a sentimental glorification of weakness of mind and degeneration of character."

Notably, the initially critical reception did not affect the novel's popularity, and later critics were farmore accepting of the book. Indeed, in his 1986 book, *John Steinbeck's Fiction: The Aesthetics of the Road Taken*, John H. Timmerman focuses on the problems of civilization, consumerism, and nature in *Cannery Row*. Kevin Hearle, in a critique in *After The Grapes of Wrath: Essays on John Steinbeck*, suggests that despite "Steinbeck's formidable talent for describing actual places" *Cannery Row* is "profoundly concerned with the power of discourse—literary and non-literary—to shape our understanding of the world."

What Do I Read Next?

- Ernest Hemingway's 1952 novella, *The Old Man and the Sea*, like *Cannery Row*, is a story of a man isolated within and by his own powers, and of this man's relation to nature. Whereas Steinbeck contemplates the unity of all things, Hemingway explores the conflict and struggle he sees as being at the heart of survival.

- Steinbeck's 1939 novel about the Dust Bowl, *The Grapes of Wrath*, unlike *Cannery Row*, is one of the major social novels of the twentieth century. It also established Steinbeck as one of the greatest American writers of the twentieth century.

- The popular radio performer and author Garrison Keillor wrote *Lake Wobegon Days* (1985). Very much in the spirit of *Cannery Row*, the book weaves a number of vignettes into a portrait of a fictional town in Minnesota.

- Thornton Wilder's 1938 classic depiction of small-town America, *Our Town*, explores the organic connections between individuals and the interplay of life and death in human life.

- Elie Wiesel's memoir, *Night* (1958), relates events that were happening in the same time period as that in which *Cannery Row* takes place. *Night*, however, discusses Wiesel's experiences in the Auschwitz concentration camp, not in the more humane setting Steinbeck evokes. Nevertheless, the connection between individuals and their environment that Steinbeck seeks to explore in *Cannery Row* can also be found in Wiesel's book.

Sources

Hearle, Kevin, "'The Boat-Shaped Mind': Steinbeck's Sense of Language as Discourse in *Cannery Row* and *Sea of Cortez*," in *After The Grapes of Wrath: Essays on John Steinbeck*, edited by Donald V. Coers, Paul D. Ruffin, and Robert J. DeMott, Ohio University Press, 1995, pp. 101-12.

Lisca, Peter, *The Wide World of John Steinbeck*, Rutgers University Press, 1958, pp. 197-98.

Steinbeck John, *Cannery Row*, in *Novels, 1942-1952*, Library of America, 2001, pp. 101-225.

Timmerman, John H., *John Steinbeck's Fiction: The Aesthetics of the Road Taken*, University of Oklahoma Press, 1986, pp. 133-65.

Further Reading

Astro, Richard, *John Steinbeck and Edward F. Ricketts: The Shaping of a Novelist*, University of Minnesota Press, 1973.

> Ricketts was the model for Doc in *Cannery Row*, and the man to whom Steinbeck dedicated the novel. This book explores the relationship between Steinbeck and Ricketts.

Parini, Jay, *John Steinbeck: A Biography*, Henry Holt, 1994.

> This literary biography reconstructs Steinbeck's, life as a writer.

Riesman, David, *The Lonely Crowd*, Yale University Press, 1955.

> This landmark sociological study of the challenge to individuals living in a mass society, pays particular attention to the various adaptations possible, focusing on three particular responses that Riesman calls tradition oriented, inner directed, and outer directed, categories that well describe the characters in *Cannery Row*. Doc, for example, is an inner directed man.

Sinclair, Upton, *The Jungle*, Grosset & Dunlap, 1906.

This landmark novel focuses on the meat packing industry in Chicago at the beginning of the twentieth century. Unlike *Cannery Row*, it is not only a novel of local character but is also a work of propaganda that is meant to incite social change.

Steinbeck, John, *Steinbeck: A Life in Letters*, edited by Elaine Steinbeck and Robert Wallstein, Penguin Books, 1975.

This is an extensive, comprehensive collection of Steinbeck's letters, whether to his wife or to the president of the United States. The letters are dated from 1923 until right before Steinbeck's death.

CPSIA information can be obtained
at www.ICGtesting.com
Printed in the USA
BVHW081802090919
557952BV00015B/2117/P